THE CUT

by Mark Ravenhill

SAMUEL FRENCH

samuelfrench.co.uk

FOR AMATEUR PRODUCTION ENQUIRIES

UNITED KINGDOM AND WORLD
EXCLUDING NORTH AMERICA
plays@samuelfrench.co.uk
020 7255 4302/01

Each title is subject to availability from Samuel French,
depending upon country of performance.

THINKING ABOUT PERFORMING A SHOW?

There are thousands of plays and musicals available to perform from Samuel French right now, and applying for a licence is easier and more affordable than you might think

From classic plays to brand new musicals, from monologues to epic dramas, there are shows for everyone.

Plays and musicals are protected by copyright law, so if you want to perform them, the first thing you'll need is a licence. This simple process helps support the playwright by ensuring they get paid for their work and means that you'll have the documents you need to stage the show in public.

Not all our shows are available to perform all the time, so it's important to check and apply for a licence before you start rehearsals or commit to doing the show.

LEARN MORE & FIND THOUSANDS OF SHOWS

Browse our full range of plays and musicals, and find out more about how to license a show

www.samuelfrench.co.uk/perform

Talk to the friendly experts in our Licensing team for advice on choosing a show and help with licensing

plays@samuelfrench.co.uk   020 7387 9373

Acting Editions

BORN TO PERFORM

Playscripts designed from the ground up to work the way you do in rehearsal, performance and study

---

Larger, clearer text for easier reading

Wider margins for notes

Performance features such as character and props lists, sound and lighting cues, and more

---

+ CHOOSE A SIZE AND STYLE TO SUIT YOU

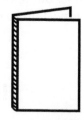

STANDARD EDITION

Our regular paperback book at our regular size

SPIRAL-BOUND EDITION

The same size as the Standard Edition, but with a sturdy, easy-to-fold, easy-to-hold spiral-bound spine

LARGE EDITION

A4 size and spiral bound, with larger text and a blank page for notes opposite every page of text – perfect for technical and directing use

LEARN MORE | **samuelfrench.co.uk/actingeditions**

MUSIC USE NOTE

Licensees are solely responsible for obtaining formal written permission from copyright owners to use copyrighted music in the performance of this play and are strongly cautioned to do so. If no such permission is obtained by the licensee, then the licensee must use only original music that the licensee owns and controls. Licensees are solely responsible and liable for all music clearances and shall indemnify the copyright owners of the play(s) and their licensing agent, Samuel French, against any costs, expenses, losses and liabilities arising from the use of music by licensees. Please contact the appropriate music licensing authority in your territory for the rights to any incidental music.

IMPORTANT BILLING AND CREDIT REQUIREMENTS

If you have obtained performance rights to this title, please refer to your licensing agreement for important billing and credit requirements.

Other plays by MARK RAVENHILL
published and licensed by Samuel French

Candide

Citizenship

Ghost Story

Golden Child

Handbag

Mother Clap's Molly House

Over There

Pool (No Water)

Product

Scenes from Family Life

Shoot/Get Treasure/Repeat

Shopping and Fucking

Some Explicit Polaroids

The Experiment

FIND PERFECT PLAYS TO PERFORM AT
www.samuelfrench.co.uk/perform

ABOUT THE AUTHOR

Mark Ravenhill was born in Haywards Heath, West Sussex in 1966. He studied Drama and English at Bristol University. His first play *Shopping and Fucking* was produced by Out of Joint and the Royal Court Theatre in 1996. Subsequent plays include *Faust Is Dead* and *Handbag* (both Actors Touring Company), *Some Explicit Polaroids* (Out of Joint at the Ambassadors Theatre), *Mother Clap's Molly House* and *Citizenship* (both National Theatre), *Pool (No Water)* (Frantic Assembly at the Lyric Theatre), *The Cut* (Donmar Theatre), *Shoot/Get Treasure/Repeat* (Paines Plough) and *Over There* (Royal Court). From 2012 to 2014, Mark was playwright in residence for the Royal Shakespeare Company, producing a new version of Brecht's *Galileo* and a new play *Candide* inspired by Voltaire (both Swan Theatre, Stratford-Upon-Avon). Mark's work in music theatre includes a new English version of Monteverdi's *The Coronation of Poppea* with additional material by Michael Nyman (King's Head); *Ten Plagues*, a song cycle for Marc Almond with composer Connor Mitchell (Traverse Theatre) and *Elysium* with composer Rolf Wallin for the Norwegian Opera. Mark is the co-creator of the ITV sitcom *Vicious*.

The Cut premiered at the Donmar Warehouse, London, on 23 February 2006.

The play is dedicated to the memory of Tim Fraser

CHARACTERS

PAUL

JOHN

GITA

SUSAN

MINA

STEPHEN

Scene One

A room. A desk. PAUL *and* JOHN.

PAUL Were the searches made?

JOHN I was searched, yes.

PAUL Was there any unnecessary brutality?

JOHN No. No, I wouldn't say it was unnecessary brutality.

PAUL Because I need to record any cases of unnecessary... I'm compiling a dossier. Which many people are eager to read.

JOHN I see.

PAUL The last lot were very slack on unnecessary brutality. Blind eyes were turned. You remember?

JOHN Yes.

PAUL But we intend to be different. We're shining a light on... We're coming down, very hard. You see? On unnecessary...

JOHN Yes.

PAUL But we need the figures, so if you were in any way...

JOHN No, no.

PAUL You have to tell me.

JOHN No.

PAUL Look to you I know I'm – what? – I'm Authority. Power. Strength. The Father.

JOHN Well—

PAUL But honestly you must tell me if there was any unnecessary – for the dossier.

JOHN No.

PAUL You're quite sure?

JOHN Very sure.

PAUL Well, that's good. Good. Good. No fist?

JOHN No.

PAUL No boot?

JOHN No.

PAUL Good. Good. Good.

> *Beat.*

> You were searched?

JOHN Yes.

PAUL Thoroughly?

JOHN Yes.

PAUL But in such a way as not to...

JOHN Yes, yes, yes.

PAUL Good, good, good. You understand why we have to...?

JOHN Of course.

PAUL Someone did actually pull a gun on me recently. Little bastard actually got a gun through and pulled it out on me.

JOHN Shit.

PAUL And fired.

JOHN Shit.

PAUL I actually saw the bullet coming out of the gun, saw it coming towards me and ducked. Just in time.

JOHN Shit.

PAUL So as you can imagine I gave those guys out there merry hell. "Security? Security? Call yourself security and you let some fucker through with a gun?" We've had to set a new target for performance. Utterly thorough without any unnecessary brutality. Using that performance indicator, how would you say the operatives did? In your experience?

JOHN Well...

PAUL Excellentverygoodgoodaveragepoor?

JOHN Very good.

PAUL So – some room for improvement. But...getting there. Good.

PAUL *records this in a file.*

Now. Can I give you any more information?

JOHN No. I don't think so.

PAUL You've read the leaflets?

JOHN I've read everything.

PAUL Well...good, good. Very...impressive.

JOHN I've been preparing for this moment for a long time. Books. The clips. I've thought about this.

PAUL Good.

JOHN I wanted to be ready.

PAUL Excellent.

JOHN I really wanted to be ready for the Cut.

PAUL Yes. Yes. Well, we'll have to see if...

JOHN Where are the instruments?

PAUL They're with—

JOHN Only in the clips they have the instruments all laid out, you know. On the desk. There. Before I...before he...walks into the room they're all laid out and then "are you ready for the Cut?", "Yes". And – instruments in and—

PAUL Pain.

JOHN Pain and then – done.

PAUL Yes, well – that was the last lot. All very brutal. All very fast. We're...different.

JOHN Yes?

PAUL Oh yes. We're very different. We've made some changes.

JOHN Oh. I see.

PAUL We're a force for change. So...let's consider some other options.

JOHN No.

PAUL We're going to look at—

JOHN No.

PAUL No?

JOHN I want to... I'm here for the Cut. I want the Cut. That's what I'm here for. The Cut.

PAUL And I'm here to look at the options. And as I'm...as I'm this side of the desk, we're going to look at the options. We're going to look at your choices. Alright?

JOHN Alright.

PAUL There's a prison facility. We offer a prison facility to the insane. Are you insane?

JOHN No.

PAUL Because if you're insane—

JOHN I'm not insane.

PAUL Although prison doesn't come cheap. You pay. Or – poverty pending – we pay. So nobody's keen on the prison facility. Still, if you're actually insane—

JOHN I'm not.

PAUL Do you have the paperwork?

JOHN Here.

JOHN *hands* PAUL *a piece of paper.*

PAUL Well, this all seems to be... So you're actually sane?

JOHN Yes.

PAUL Well, that's very impressive. In this day and age. Now, there's the army. Let's think about that.

JOHN No.

PAUL Or the university. Maybe we should be sending you to the university.

JOHN No, no. I don't want—

PAUL The army and the university. Much more cost-efficient than prison. Let's talk about—

JOHN No, no, let's not. Let's not mess about.

PAUL Mess about?

JOHN Mess about. This, this, this... You're the man who does the Cut, right?

PAUL I'm in the office of the building where the Cut is—

JOHN Then do the Cut. Do the Cut on me.

PAUL This is the office. This is the building. But that doesn't have to define...me. You. We have choices. You and me. We can be... There's the army, the university, the prison. So much choice.

JOHN No, no.

PAUL Oh, oh, would you rather be under the last lot?

JOHN No, no, no.

PAUL Because if you're telling me you'd rather be under the last lot then that, my son, is a political statement, and if you're making political statements, if you're standing here in a public place – and yes, this is classified as a public place – standing in a public space and making political statements then it's the university for you. I'll send you straight off to the university and they'll soon put a stop to these political statements.

JOHN No, no, no. I wasn't... There wasn't anything political, just...

PAUL Yes?

JOHN Just I've got this far, you know?

PAUL Of course.

JOHN Always another office, always another interview, another search, another form to fill. From my village to the town to the city and now...now that I've got this far I thought you'd just...just...

PAUL Yes?

JOHN I thought you were a rubber stamp.

PAUL I am more, I am much much much more than a rubber as you put it stamp.

JOHN Of course.

PAUL Would I have all this space, all this facility, all this... fucking impressive... How do I look to you...?

JOHN Well, yes, impressive.

PAUL And?

JOHN And, and...

PAUL And?

JOHN Old. As in wise. As in responsible. As in, as in, as in, as in...

PAUL Authority.

JOHN Authoritative.

PAUL As in authoritative authority. Yes. As in burdened with, the burden of...

JOHN Exactly.

PAUL Do you think I tell my wife what I do here? (I have a wife). Do you think my children...? (One's in prison – expensive – one's in university – cheaper.) Do you think I tell my children what I do here? Have you thought about that?

JOHN Well, maybe you should. Maybe you should. Maybe. Because, listen, the Cut, I think it's... I want the Cut. I think the Cut's a very beautiful...a very old and beautiful... It's a ritual, a custom, something we...

PAUL I don't think so.

JOHN To actually leave your body.

PAUL Have you any idea of the suffering? The pain? The great screams as the instruments go in?

JOHN Of course.

PAUL They claw at me. They howl at the sky. It's barbaric.

JOHN I know all that. All the clips. But I want—

PAUL And I have to carry all this on. Disgusting. You know we actually – off the record – have a working party looking at, considering ending the whole thing.

JOHN No.

PAUL Off the record.

JOHN Why?

PAUL Progress. Humanity. Etcetera. Our core values.

JOHN But that's centuries of...you can't wipe out centuries of... my grandmother, my uncles, so many centuries—

PAUL You can't stand in the way of core values. None of us can.

JOHN Everybody had the Cut.

PAUL And for now of course we're carrying it through.

JOHN Good.

PAUL Just...softening the blow. Talking. We get to know you. You get to know us.

JOHN How does that...?

PAUL For the records.

JOHN Please. I'd like to see the instruments. I don't want to talk.

PAUL I'll be the judge—

JOHN This isn't right. This isn't how it's supposed to be. I'm not supposed to get to know you. You're not supposed to talk to me. You're just supposed to show me the instruments.

PAUL New procedures.

JOHN I haven't heard about—

PAUL There's new procedures all the time. Every day practically. Only this morning I received a directive.

JOHN Where do you keep the instruments?

PAUL New guidelines for talking. Keep things inclusive.

JOHN I don't want to talk.

PAUL If you want to see the directive—

JOHN I'm not going to talk.

PAUL Box files full of the things. Aims. Objectives. Targets. Outcomes. Let me show them. We're very open. It's a root and branch thing.

JOHN No. No. No. Just – Cut me. Come on. Do it. Do it. Show me the instruments. Get the instruments and Cut me.

PAUL Just – like that – cruel, cold, hard, impersonal?

JOHN Yes yes yes.

PAUL That would make me very unhappy. You'd be in great pain—

JOHN I know that.

PAUL But also I'd be in great pain. Inside. Enormous pain – physical for you, spiritual for me.

JOHN Yes. Please. Come on. It's what I want. Fuck's sake –
that's what I want.

PAUL Are you sure you're not insane?

JOHN You've seen the paperwork—

PAUL And I suppose we'll have to take their word but still I've
never seen anybody so...keen.

JOHN Yes well...

PAUL So keen for the Cut. Why are you—?

JOHN I don't want to talk.

PAUL Just a little longer.

JOHN I'd rather we just—

PAUL Tell me. Tell me and I'll show you the instruments.

JOHN You've got them?

PAUL Of course I've got them. Couldn't be in my position unless
I had the instruments, could I?

JOHN Then where...?

PAUL Ah.

JOHN In the desk? There's a special drawer in the—?

PAUL No. Stuffed to the brim with directives. The girl. The girl
has the instruments.

JOHN The girl?

PAUL Gita. Did you see Gita on your way in?

JOHN No.

PAUL Well, yes, easily missed, Gita. Can't speak. Can't hear. It's
a condition. But we found her a place. Inclusion.

JOHN Tell her to bring the instruments in.

PAUL She may be—

JOHN Tell her to bring the instrument or I won't talk.

PAUL *goes to a door, opens it, beckons. Enter* GITA.

PAUL You're looking very good today, Gita. We're almost ready. We've almost finished talking and we're almost ready for the instruments. Could you get them ready, Gita? Thank you.

Exit GITA.

She's very good. Back in a minute. So – tell me. Tell me why you're so different.

JOHN Am I?

PAUL Oh yes. Totally different. I've never seen...normally I see fear, anger. Sometimes...sullen, nothing. But you're keen. Because...?

JOHN Because. Because I want to be free. Free of, of, of me. Of all this. I want it to be Cut away. I want to be Cut away from this body. Yes – and this history and this wanting and this busyness and this schooling and these, these ties. I want to be released.

PAUL And you think ?/ You really think?

JOHN Yes yes.

PAUL You think that's what the Cut—?

JOHN I know. I know that's what the Cut does.

PAUL You're very idealistic.

JOHN I don't think so.

PAUL Bit of a dreamer.

JOHN No.

PAUL Yes, dreamer. Because, look...wouldn't we all? Wouldn't we all like—?

JOHN We can.

PAUL We'd all like to be free. Believe me, I want to be free of bodies, of history, of wanting... I'd like that just as much as...

JOHN Then...free yourself.

PAUL I can't.

JOHN You can. Anybody can.

PAUL No. No. I Cut. You are Cut. That's my burden. Nobody's ever changed that—

JOHN But if you—

PAUL We can stop Cutting. But we'll still be the people who used to Cut. You'll still be the people who used to be Cut. Always the same. No fucking point. We soften the blow. Maybe we end the Cut. But still the old circles, the old divides. Young and I thought – change it all. I can make it all better. Nothing's going to be the same. Out with the last lot. And now look at me. Repellent. Can't tell my beautiful wife, my beautiful children—

JOHN Listen, listen, listen.

PAUL What does it matter? Send my beautiful children to the prison or the university, still they'll be...

JOHN Listen to me.

PAUL They'll always be Cutters, never Cut.

JOHN I want to show you.

PAUL The old lot, the new lot. Everything's the same. We've changed nothing.

JOHN Shhhh. Shhhh. I've got something to show you.

PAUL Yes?

JOHN Yes. I've discovered... I want to share... I always knew what the Cut was going to be, okay?

PAUL Alright.

JOHN Liberty. Freedom. Nothingness. I knew that. Don't ask me how. But from dot I knew, so I...

PAUL Yes?

JOHN Prepared myself. Practised little moments of emptiness. Not forever like the Cut but moments. And you can do that.

PAUL I can't.

JOHN You can. Each of us can. Each and every one of us can free ourselves.

PAUL Not me.

JOHN If only you'll...shut your eyes.

PAUL No.

JOHN Please.

PAUL No. I'm sorry. But you understand. After the incident. With the gun. After the incident with the gun I find trust impossible.

JOHN Of course.

PAUL Which has made lovemaking with my wife, which has made it – does this embarrass you?

JOHN No no.

PAUL Which has made lovemaking with my wife impossible. It's only when you can't...when you can no longer close your eyes during the, the, the...act that you realise...lovemaking with the eyes wide open...impossible.

JOHN I see.

PAUL Unnerving for her, embarrassing for me.

JOHN Of course. I've been searched.

PAUL But if you strangled me.

JOHN Beat me away. Beat me to the ground. Beat me to death. I'm weak. You're strong. You can easily beat me.

PAUL Yes yes I suppose I can.

JOHN But I'm not going to strangle you.

PAUL No?

JOHN No. Now please. The eyes.

PAUL *closes his eyes.*

Long silence.

And there's total darkness.

PAUL Well, almost.

JOHN Please don't speak. That's vital. It's vital that you don't speak.

PAUL I understand.

JOHN Ahhah. Total darkness. And you have no body. Your body has dissolved. Dissolved or melted away. Every piece of skin or bone or hair. Every last cell gone away. The cage has vanished. And you are free.

Feel the darkness. Feel the void.

Remember how they used to scare you with that? Remember then how you used to scare yourself with that?

The darkness. Where the monsters live. Where the witches live. Where the paedophiles are. The darkness. Don't go into the darkness. Carry the candle. Leave a light in the window. Take a torch into the woods.

Lies. All of it lies.

The void. It'll eat you up. The chasm that swallows the sailors, swallows the ships, swallows the astronauts. The hole, the pit, the gap. Avoid. Avoid. Avoid. Take a map, make a rope bridge. Steer clear of the void.

Lies lies all of it lies.

They've told you lies and you've kept your eyes open. When all freedom asked of you was to close your eyes.

And now you've closed them. And you've made a start.

But still you're trying to work out where the light switch is. Still the torch is in your hand. Still you're fingering the switch. In case. In case. In case.

Don't. Please. I beg you. Spin around. Spin around until you're dizzy and there's no light switch. Let the torch fall from your hand. Let it roll away into the forest. Let the mud suck it up and rot it away.

And stand in the darkness. And become the darkness.

The truth.

And feel everything go.

There's no history. All that struggling to move forward, to expand, to progress. That's gone away.

And there's no society. All the prisons and the universities have fallen down or been exploded. Or maybe they never were. It doesn't matter.

The truth.

And your wife and your children. Eaten away by cancers or burnt to nothing or maybe never born. Generation after generation never born. Back and back until the first stroke of the first day of the first time. None of it ever was.

The truth.

And so there's nothing.

Don't fight. Don't try and feel your body. Don't reach for the reports. Don't try and call your wife.

Because it's all nothing.

There's only truth. There's only you.

Darkness is light. Void is everything. You are truth.

Long silence.

And open your eyes

And open your eyes

And open your eyes

PAUL I don't want to.

JOHN Open them.

PAUL No.

JOHN I've got a gun. In my hand. Pointing at you. I'm squeezing the trigger.

PAUL *opens his eyes.*

Sorry. I had to—

PAUL No gun? No gun? Where's the fucking gun? You said there was a—

JOHN Yes because you wouldn't—

PAUL Listen, son, don't fuck around. If there's a gun then have a fucking gun, okay? Okay? Okay?

JOHN I was just trying.

PAUL Fuck. I wanted to... I didn't want to open my... Why did you make...?

JOHN Because it's not healthy.

PAUL Healthy? Healthy? Healthy? Fuck you. Fuck you. Fuck you. Sorry. Sorry. Sorry.

Pause.

I'm sorry. I really wanted... I just wanted you to shoot...

JOHN It was a tactic.

PAUL Really thought you'd shoot me. That's what I wanted. I wanted to be shot with my eyes shut.

JOHN I wouldn't do that.

PAUL But then – cunt that I am – I opened my eyes. Fucked up. Because I'm – what? – a coward. And you – cunt – no gun. We're both cunts. Everyone's cunts. Everything's a cunt. The whole shebang is one big fucking cunting cunty cunt.

JOHN No no.

PAUL Because that's what you're...preaching, isn't it? In your... sermon.

JOHN I don't use words like that.

PAUL But you are. That's what you're saying. Everything's shit. Everything's fucked up. There's nothing worth crap.

JOHN No no.

PAUL We've tried everything and it's all a void. That's what you said.

JOHN No I didn't. No I didn't.

PAUL Yes you did. Please don't correct me. I know. I know. What were you doing? Talking. Blah. Blah. Blah. But I. I was listening. With my eyes shut. And I know what I heard.

JOHN From your perspective.

PAUL The truth. Everything's finished. Everything's over. We're all done.

JOHN You're twisting everything—

PAUL Listen, son. I'm old. I'm wise. You gibber. I shift the shit and pick out the gems. Okay? Okay? Okay?

JOHN Okay.

PAUL And you're right. And I admire you. I revere you. To say what's been in my head, what I've never been able to... The articulation. Because as you said I was afraid and I have been lied to. For generations.

And there in the dark. In the moment. I saw. I'm worthless.

I'm a piece of shit. I'm a speck of shit on a lump of shit on a piece of shit. I'm nothing.

And I don't want to carry on.

And I do have...

PAUL *produces a gun.*

Shoot me.

JOHN No.

PAUL As an act of kindness.

JOHN No. I'm not an emotional—

PAUL Yes yes yes. Go. Off you go.

JOHN No.

PAUL It's going to get very bloody in here. I'm going for the head. Blood and brains all over the place. And I don't want you to be a part of that.

JOHN You mustn't.

PAUL Here. I'll stamp your report. Show it to the girl on the desk. She'll give you your travel money home. We pay reasonable second class fares. Go back to your village – I take it you have a village and a, and a family.

JOHN No.

PAUL Alright. You might want to stand back. Blood in your hair and so on.

JOHN Don't be so...don't be so...no no no. I'm here. I'm here for the Cut. That's what I'm here for. That's what you're supposed to do. You're supposed to administer the Cut.

PAUL I'm supposed to...

JOHN That's your duty. That's your calling. That's why you were chosen.

PAUL Yes well, I'm...

JOHN And that's why I'm here. That's what I've waited so long for. This is what I've been planning for.

PAUL I'm sorry. Things change.

JOHN No no no. The clips, the books, waiting, waiting, planning, planning. Every moment I ever lived for this moment, you can't oh please oh please oh please oh please oh please...

PAUL There's a tear.

JOHN Yes.

PAUL You've got a tear.

JOHN Yes.

PAUL That's very emotional...

JOHN I know. Sorry. Sorry. Where's Gita? Where are the instruments?

PAUL They're being sterilised.

JOHN Please. Bring them in.

PAUL We have to reuse them. Public finances. But also sterilise them. Public health.

JOHN I understand. Please. Show me the instruments.

PAUL You're a very selfish young man.

JOHN Yes.

PAUL To ride roughshod over my suffering.

JOHN I know, I know.

PAUL Have you any idea of the burden for a man – of my class?

JOHN No.

PAUL No no you don't. Very well.

PAUL *rings a bell.*

JOHN Thank you.

PAUL This evening I shall eat a meal with my wife. We have drinks first. Then a meal. Then I shall read. Then I'll – we'll sleep in a bed. With my wife. But all the time I'll be suffering. Like nobody can believe. And I'll wake up tomorrow. And I'll say: Today I'll shoot myself. That kid who got the Cut was right. I should shoot myself.

JOHN Are the instruments...?

PAUL Coming. The kid was right. I should shoot myself. But I won't. Oh, I'll look at the gun. I'll handle it. All day long under the desk I'll be handling the gun. But I won't fire. I won't fire tomorrow or the next day or the next day or the next day or the next day. Or never. I'll be permanently not shooting myself. Can you imagine the horror of that? No you can't. Of course you can't. You. You. You...shit.

Enter GITA, *carrying the instruments.*

Ah, Gita, thank you, thank you. Gita's just joined us. She's still training but she's doing very well. Down there, Gita.

GITA *places the instruments down and steps back.*

JOHN Can I touch them?

PAUL Well, it's not a regular...

JOHN Please.

PAUL Of course. No, no, Gita. It's alright. Stay.

JOHN *picks up the instruments.*

JOHN These are...twenty-three years old.

PAUL Public finances. Lack of investment.

JOHN From a workshop in the north. The north-western workshop.

PAUL Very impressive.

JOHN Look at them. Just look.

PAUL I'm afraid they're purely functional to me.

JOHN No no no. Classic craftsmanship. This is an honour. Thank you. Thank you.

PAUL Shall we get on with it?

JOHN Yes.

PAUL Gita.

GITA *comes forward.*

I envy you. I envy everything about you. If you could give me a word. Just a word so I can shoot myself.

JOHN No.

PAUL You've broken me.

JOHN I didn't mean to.

PAUL That doesn't make it any fucking better. Gita. The lights.

GITA *switches off the lights. Total darkness.*

You are here for the Cut. Please prepare yourself for the Cut.

Long, long pause.

I don't want to...

JOHN You have to.

PAUL Please, I can't...

JOHN Now. Do it now.

PAUL Fuck it. Fuck it. Fuck it. The Cut is about to take place.

Long, long pause. **JOHN** *gasps as the instruments go in.*

JOHN Thank you. Thank you. Thank you.

Scene Two

PAUL's *flat.* PAUL *and* SUSAN.

SUSAN She's like a child. Quite honestly like a simple little child. I walk in and she's looking at it boiling over. Actually standing there and watching – just...watching as it's boiling over. And I say, "Mina – the soup's boiling over" and she says, "Yes miss" and then she carries on, carries on looking.

PAUL Mmmmm.

SUSAN And I suppose I should have been angry. I suppose angry would have been an altogether appropriate response. Would you have been angry?

PAUL Well...

SUSAN I think you might have been. I think you might have flown into one of your rages.

PAUL Well...

SUSAN Oh yes, I can see you now tearing into her. Just tearing straight into her.

PAUL I don't know.

SUSAN But somehow I...I...I smiled, maybe – I think I laughed a bit, I indulged...yes, alright, I indulged...and I said, "maybe if you took it off the... You see?"

PAUL Mmmmmmm...

SUSAN And she did. She did when I actually told her what to do.

PAUL Well, good.

SUSAN But of course tomorrow we'll be right back to square one. She'll be watching it boil over all over again. Little goldfish.

PAUL Yes.

SUSAN It's a great pressure on me. This watching. All the time watching, guiding. There's a burden.

PAUL Of course.

SUSAN Sometimes half an hour with her... I have to lie down. In the dark. For several hours.

PAUL We could have her reassigned.

SUSAN I went to the hospital.

PAUL Shall I look into having her reassigned?

SUSAN I went to the hospital. But really I was fobbed off. A few tablets. They're useless.

PAUL Let's get her reassigned.

SUSAN And can you imagine the fuss?

PAUL There needn't be a fuss.

SUSAN You haven't seen the family. You're never here when the... Oh there's a father. And a mother. And a brother. I suspect that she has a child.

PAUL Really?

SUSAN I suspect. Just a... And they'll all be round here crying and pleading and looking and...

PAUL Really? Really? Really?

SUSAN You don't know. You just don't know. Oh yes. I don't think I can handle the fuss.

PAUL So we'll keep her?

SUSAN I don't know. I don't know. I suppose. I suppose we must. I suppose I'll just have to do the best I can.

PAUL You're a remarkable person.

SUSAN Thank you.

PAUL No. I mean it. You're a remarkable person. And I appreciate what you do. For us.

SUSAN Supper will be late.

PAUL I just want you to know...you're valued.

SUSAN After the soup and everything...there'll be a wait for supper.

PAUL Ah well.

SUSAN So just try...try not to get angry until the food arrives.

PAUL I'm not going to...

SUSAN I know you, I know you. Your blood sugar...if the blood sugar's not even that's when you start to get...

PAUL What? What?

SUSAN You get tetchy.

PAUL No. No. No.

SUSAN It's always the same. Yes. Yes. Yes. You're always the same. So just hold on.

PAUL You know me.

SUSAN Oh yes.

PAUL You know me very well.

SUSAN I know you totally.

PAUL Ah.

SUSAN I know you absolutely and totally.

PAUL Yes. Yes. Is that boring?

SUSAN Darling...

PAUL A man with no secrets?

SUSAN Darling.

PAUL Is it dull to have no doors left to open?

SUSAN It's...comfortable. I'd say we're comfortable. Wouldn't you say we're comfortable?

PAUL Yes.

SUSAN Yes. Comfortable's the word.

PAUL But physically...

SUSAN You know there's a big push now. From the universities. I got a letter from Stephen.

PAUL Mmmmm?

SUSAN Today. Stephen wrote from the university. He's looking forward to his fruit cake. Stephen wrote and he said there's a big push now in the universities. The students mainly. But also the lecturers. And there's a big push against the Cut.

PAUL Really?

SUSAN Yes. That's what he said.

PAUL Really?

SUSAN Yes. There's a real groundswell of...there's a real mood for ending the whole thing.

PAUL Really?

SUSAN What do you think?

PAUL If that's what Stephen—

SUSAN Yes. But what do you think?

PAUL I think, I think—

SUSAN I think they're right. I think they're absolutely...

PAUL Really? Really?

SUSAN I think these reforms, these, these, these new criteria... I mean softening the blow, I think that's... I think that's... dressing...and I think it's time...

PAUL What's he doing?

SUSAN Mmmm?

PAUL What's Stephen...?

SUSAN I don't...writing...stuff... They have papers and... discussions and... I don't...

PAUL So...talking?

SUSAN Talking and writing. Yes. Yes.

PAUL Ah. Ah. Ah. Ah. Student stuff.

SUSAN It's a start.

PAUL Is it? Is it? Is it?

SUSAN Shall I hurry her along?

PAUL What?

SUSAN Mina. Shall I hurry her along?

PAUL Why?

SUSAN You're getting tetchy. It's starting.

PAUL No.

SUSAN I can see it. The blood sugar's...dropping. There's a...
You're starting to snap.

PAUL No. No. It's just...politics.

SUSAN Yes?

PAUL It makes me uncomfortable.

SUSAN I'm sorry.

PAUL No. No. But I've...I've had a day.

SUSAN Of course.

PAUL I've had a day and all I wanted was to get back to you
and sit with you and eat and read and...

SUSAN Talk.

PAUL And talk, yes, of course talk and so of course I find it
uncomfortable...

SUSAN Of course. What did you do?

PAUL Mmmmm?

SUSAN What did you do today?

PAUL Oh. Nothing.

SUSAN You always say... Really? Really? Nothing?

PAUL Well, nothing of... Numbers, figures, reports, dossiers.

SUSAN Ah.

PAUL I've got a title. I've got an office. I've got a big office. But really, really I'm just a rubber stamp.

SUSAN No darling.

PAUL Yes really.

SUSAN No darling. I'm sure... I know you're much much much more than a rubber stamp.

PAUL No.

SUSAN I try to imagine what you do. I try to picture it. I lie on my bed in the dark in the afternoon. And Mina is breaking something. She's always breaking something in the next room. And I try to block her out. It's better now I've got the pills. And I block her out and I try to picture what you're doing.

PAUL Really?

SUSAN Really. I actually try to get a picture in my head of what you're up to.

PAUL And what do you see?

SUSAN Ah. Ah. Ah.

PAUL Come on. What do you see?

SUSAN Well, darling...

PAUL It's a pretty stupid thing to do, isn't it?

SUSAN Is it?

PAUL I should say so. Pretty stupid pointless fucking thing to do. Lying on the bed in the middle of the afternoon. What the fuck are you doing lying on the bed in the afternoon? You shouldn't be lying on the bed in the afternoon. What's wrong with you? There's nothing wrong with you. If there's anything wrong with you we'll find you a better fucking hospital. A better fucking hospital and find some pills that really do the trick.

SUSAN Hey. Hey. Hey.

PAUL But there's nothing wrong with you. There's nothing wrong. You think the world's such a bad place? You talk to Stephen and you think that the world is such a bad place then fucking do something about it.

SUSAN (going to door) Mina. Mina.

PAUL Writing. Discussions. Just fucking do something. For the losers. Take them some clothes. Go through the wardrobe and take them some clothes. Or take them some food. Bake a fucking fruit cake. Bake a hundred fucking fruit cakes and go out to the villages and give out the fruit cake. And help instead of lying on the fucking bed in the afternoon.

SUSAN Mina. I'm calling you.

PAUL I'm talking to you.

SUSAN No you're not.

PAUL Why is your life so petty? Why is your existence so utterly meaningless?

SUSAN I'll talk to Mina and we'll get the food on the table.

PAUL So meaningless that you have to imagine me at a desk in the afternoon.

SUSAN Hold your horses. The food's on its way.

PAUL I don't want the fucking food.

SUSAN Yes you do. Yes you do. Your blood sugar—

PAUL Fuck's sake.

SUSAN Has now swung into the danger zone.

PAUL Blood sugar in the danger zone? Where do you get this, where does this—?

SUSAN You're always like this. The danger zone spells tetchiness.

PAUL What is this? Some clip you've seen?

SUSAN We need to treat this as soon as we possibly can.

PAUL I'm not your patient. I'm not here for—

SUSAN Let's feed you, darling. Let's feed you and everything
will be alright.

Enter MINA.

Mina. Mina. Where is the food? The food is very late. We've
been waiting. And it's not you that suffers. It's never you
that suffers. Mister is suffering because of his blood sugar—

PAUL Agh.

SUSAN And Miss is suffering because Mister is suffering and
Mister is now tetchy. Bread straight away. Supper as soon
as you can.

MINA *Yes Miss.*

Exit MINA.

SUSAN Like a child. Look at her. Never really understands.

PAUL Will we fuck tonight?

SUSAN I don't know.

PAUL Really? Really? You don't know?

SUSAN How should I know?

PAUL Maybe because...

SUSAN It's not something we can plan for.

PAUL No.

SUSAN I would really rather that was spontaneous.

PAUL Well, let's see, we haven't...

SUSAN I'd rather that was something that just happened between
us.

PAUL It's been six months.

SUSAN Has it?

PAUL Give or take – yes, six months.

SUSAN Because, because...

PAUL So I should say...six months. At least. More like seven or eight...

SUSAN No.

PAUL Eight months. I should say the chances of a fuck tonight are pretty slim.

SUSAN Well maybe yes maybe.

PAUL I would say definitely.

SUSAN Alright then.

PAUL I would say definitely zero.

SUSAN Alright.

PAUL Why is that, do you think?

SUSAN Well, because...

PAUL Why is there nothing spontaneous happening between us?

SUSAN I should say because...because...

PAUL Why do you sleep in Stephen's old room, wait 'til you think I'm asleep then pad along the corridor to Stephen's room?

SUSAN Because...

PAUL Why have I been tossing myself to sleep for eight fucking months?

SUSAN Because you always kept your eyes closed.

PAUL Did I?

SUSAN Yes. Because your eyes were shut. Not just... Squeezed tight. From start to finish.

PAUL Crap. Crap.

SUSAN True. True. Fucking true and you know it. And you wept.

PAUL What?

SUSAN Eyes squeezed tight with great tears down your cheeks.

PAUL This is...

SUSAN Your chest holding in the...some grief. Grieving as we fucked.

PAUL No. No. No.

SUSAN Please don't... Grieving as we fucked. And eventually... as a woman...you don't...you can't...

PAUL Why do you have to spout this shit? Why do you let this crap come out of your mouth?

SUSAN I know. I saw.

PAUL Have you ever seen me cry? Do I look like a man who cries? Has there ever been a day...? Christ, we've known each other for fucking generations. Under the last lot. Under the new lot. We've been together for so fucking long. And have I ever been a crying man?

SUSAN Only when we—

PAUL So please don't give me this...because I really don't need this, this, this, this shit.

SUSAN How can you just, just—?

PAUL SHUT UP. SHUT THE FUCK UP.

Silence. Enter MINA *with bread on a plate.*

SUSAN Thank you, Mina. Did you get this from the—? Well, you better get back to the... Mina, there's a chip on this plate. Do you know anything about this chip on the side of this plate here? Listen, you'd better get back to the supper.

MINA Yes, Miss.

Exit MINA.

SUSAN Look at this. A chip on the side of the plate here. This was a new set this week. Pristine. She worked her way through the last lot. Boom. Crash. Clump. Sometimes I laugh at her. And sometimes I just block it all out.

What can you do with a child? Here – it's good bread. I got it myself from the market. Mina never gets exactly what I want. So I've started to do the shopping myself. As of this month. And actually you know it's not such a hassle. Actually sometimes it can be quite good fun bargaining. I think I'll carry on. You need to eat.

PAUL *takes a piece of bread and breaks bits off and eats them.*

It's amazing how quickly the blood sugar level goes back to normal. Just a bit of bread. One of those little miracles. Would you like to read Stephen's letter? He wrote to me. But I'm sure he wouldn't mind – I think he'd be happy if you read it.

PAUL I love you.

SUSAN I put the letter down somewhere.

PAUL I love you.

SUSAN I was reading it – I was here...and then I got distracted by Mina and I went to the... Letter in my hand.

PAUL I love you.

SUSAN And then I was on the bed in the dark.

PAUL I love you.

SUSAN And then back in...

PAUL I love you.

SUSAN So it must be – unless she's moved it of course, which is entirely possible...

PAUL I love you.

SUSAN No. No. Here. Here.

PAUL What?

SUSAN Stephen's letter. Do you want to read it?

PAUL Thank you.

> PAUL *takes the letter.*

He's always liked fruit cake.

SUSAN Always.

PAUL Can you remember a time when he didn't like fruit cake?

SUSAN No. No. I can't.

PAUL Maybe that's why he's always been so happy. Blood sugar's up, eh?

SUSAN Yes, maybe that's it.

PAUL I think he's wasting his time.

SUSAN Mmmmm?

PAUL Writing. Discussing. Never change anything.

SUSAN Not immediately.

PAUL And then you... They actually want it, you know?

SUSAN They?

PAUL They want to be Cut.

SUSAN Hardly.

PAUL Oh yes, you listen to them. On the bus or...they actually want it.

SUSAN They can't want to.

PAUL You realise the tradition, the...it actually means something. It gives them meaning.

SUSAN No. No.

PAUL That's the reality of the situation.

SUSAN How do you know?

PAUL I overhear, I observe.

SUSAN How can you say that?

PAUL Because I am actually out there, day after day. I actually—

SUSAN And I'm... I go shopping. I go outside too.

PAUL Yes?

SUSAN And I don't overhear... So you actually want this to go on? You don't want anything to change? You want this practice this well frankly barbaric you just want this to go on and on and on?

PAUL I'm tired.

SUSAN Are you actually defending—?

PAUL I'd love to talk to you. I'd love to debate with you. That would be a great pleasure. But actually after a day of work—

SUSAN As I see it – Stephen says...you've actually got to be for it or against it.

PAUL Grow up.

SUSAN That's what Stephen says.

PAUL Fuck's sake – Stephen is a child. Stephen is a student.

SUSAN And I think I actually agree with him.

PAUL But you – you're a grown, you're a mature, you're an old, older woman, person, I think it's a bit late to be seeing the world in—

SUSAN I think I may join a group.

PAUL Black and white. Goodies and Baddies. Us and Them. We Cut. They are cut. Fucking simplistic fucking—

SUSAN Or I may start yes actually I may start a group.

PAUL Life isn't simple. Things aren't simple. Don't simplify – let Stephen – fine, he's a student – maybe at the university but don't simplify—

SUSAN You know what I saw this afternoon?

PAUL That's all I'm saying.

SUSAN I lay on the bed this afternoon. In the dark. I took three
pills. You're only supposed to take two but I felt... I knew
those plates were vulnerable and I was feeling... Anyway
I took three tablets and I lie back on the bed, I lay back in
the darkness and I tried to picture you...

PAUL Listen...

SUSAN Which I've been doing quite a lot recently. The last –
oooo – six months. Lie on the bed in the afternoon and I try
to picture what you're doing at your office.

PAUL Don't.

SUSAN And often I get no picture at all. Often actually my
mind's still here. And I'm anxious for the crockery and the
ornaments and the windows with Mina on the loose. No
pictures at all or sometimes a picture, very dull. You're filing.
Writing down some numbers. Few seconds of a very dull
picture. That's all it's been before.

PAUL Yes.

SUSAN But today. But today. A very clear picture. Suddenly.
And you're Cutting. There's a young man. And there's the
instruments. And you're Cutting him.

PAUL Yes.

SUSAN In your dull little office you were doing the Cut. And
I wonder why did that come into my head?

PAUL Why do you think?

SUSAN I don't know. It was so clear.

PAUL Were you awake?

SUSAN Oh yes. I was looking at the ceiling. Because I noticed
a mark. Maybe it was Stephen's letter? Do you think that
put the idea into my head.

PAUL That's possible.

SUSAN That's the only thing that I can think of. Can you think of anything else?

PAUL The bread's all finished.

SUSAN There's more. Mina will bring it.

PAUL I think I've had enough. I find sometimes...I get bloated.

SUSAN You never said.

PAUL Oh yes. More than a couple of slices I find I have a tendency to get bloated.

SUSAN You never told me that before.

PAUL It's a tiny, it's a small thing...

SUSAN Maybe if we tried another...

PAUL It's only really started. In the last six months or so.

SUSAN I see. I see. These things are sent to try us, aren't they?

PAUL I suppose that's right. Yes. These things are sent to try us. I thought of you this afternoon.

SUSAN Really?

PAUL Physically. I thought about you physically this afternoon.

SUSAN We'll try another kind of bread.

PAUL And I resolved... I'd like us to try again...physically I'd like us to have another go.

SUSAN Oh.

PAUL I'd like us to pick up where we left off. Lovemaking.

SUSAN That's what you did in your office? Thought about us lovemaking?

PAUL Yes, yes I did.

SUSAN That was rather naughty.

PAUL Yes yes it was.

SUSAN And here was I. Lying in the bed. Seeing you do the Cut.

PAUL Well.

SUSAN Well.

Enter **MINA** *with a tray with two main courses and cutlery.*

Thank you, Mina. Better late than... There's a good girl. On the table.

MINA *lays the table.*

That's it, very good. Do you have a little girl or a little boy, Mina? Which is it? Boy or a girl? I tease her about it all day long. Don't I, Mina? Boy or girl, Mina? Boy or a girl? But she won't tell. You keep your secrets, don't you, Mina? You keep your cards close to your chest. But you've got a little kiddy tucked away at home. I know you do. I've got an instinct. There are no secrets from me, are there? I reckon a boy. We've got two boys. Do you want your boy to have the Cut, Mina? Like his ancestors. Course you don't. Makes you scared. Makes you angry. The Cut. Doesn't it, Mina? Well, don't you worry, Mina. Because that's all going to end. That's all going to change. My son's working on that. I'm working on that. We're going to get rid of the Cut. We're going to hunt them down and chuck them out. There'll be none of them left. There'll be none of them doing the Cut by the time your boy's a man. You'll see. You'll see. Yes. You've done very well. You've done beautifully. Oh, Mina – tomorrow, remind me when I go shopping – we're going to try a new type of bread. Mister is getting bloated so we're going to change the bread. Thank you. You go home. There's a kid waiting for you. Boy or girl, Mina? Boy or girl?

Exit **MINA**. **SUSAN** *sits at the table.*

Well, this looks pretty good. Once she gets the job done, you know, she actually does it rather well. It's just getting her there that's the challenge. I bet you're hungry. Let's start. Darling. Let's start.

PAUL I...

SUSAN I chose all the ingredients myself.

PAUL I...

SUSAN Bargained for every last bit of this.

PAUL I...

SUSAN Meals have tasted better since I did the shopping.

PAUL I, I, I, I, I, I, I... *(cries)* ...I, I, I, I, I, I, I... *(cries)*

SUSAN You always feel better after you've eaten.

PAUL I, I, I, I, I, I, I... *(cries/howls)*

SUSAN Darling. Darling. Darling.

PAUL A, A, A, A... *(cries/howls)*

SUSAN You've never been the sort of man who cries. All the time
I've known you. The last lot. The new lot. The generations.
You've never been the sort that cries. How can I make love
to you? How can I make love to a man who cries? Who
shuts his eyes and just cries and cries.

PAUL I'm...sorry.

SUSAN Well, of course you're sorry. We're all sorry. But we still
have to eat.

PAUL I don't want this. I don't want...

SUSAN Look at you. Look at you. Get up. You disgust me. You
disgust me when you're like this.

PAUL Why can't I shoot myself?

SUSAN That's a self-indulgence. There are children.

PAUL Why do we do this day after day after day?

SUSAN I don't know. Because we have to. There are things in
this world we just have to do. There are responsibilities.

PAUL Don't you ever cry?

SUSAN No. No. No. Not that I remember. Not even this afternoon.
Not even when I thought of you...no.

PAUL I'm sorry. Sorry. I won't do it again.

SUSAN You won't...?

PAUL There'll be no more tears.

SUSAN Well, that's good. Shall we eat?

PAUL Yes. Let's eat.

They sit up at the table.

SUSAN Tomorrow is fruit cake day. Baking for Stephen tomorrow. What will you be doing tomorrow.?

PAUL Same as always.

SUSAN So I shall be very busy. No time for a lie-down tomorrow. No time to think about you.

PAUL That's good.

SUSAN Yes that's good. Isn't it? That's good.

PAUL I love you.

SUSAN And then the next day we can drive to the university.

PAUL No. Please listen. Please listen to me. I love you. And I want... I wish I could show you all of myself. I wish I could let you into... I wish there was no...

SUSAN Secrets?

PAUL Barriers. I wish there were no barriers.

SUSAN Yes. Maybe that would be better.

PAUL But I can't.

SUSAN No?

PAUL I want to protect you. I want to protect us. The comfort.

SUSAN And is that working? Is...this...the answer?

PAUL I don't know. Will you stay in the bed with me – all night?

SUSAN If that's what you'd like.

PAUL I'd like that very much.

SUSAN Alright then. Alright. That's what we'll do.

PAUL I think if we just lie together for a night. If we could lie together in the dark and, and, and hold each other then that could be a start.

SUSAN Do you have a greasy fork?

PAUL It's a very small thing but I think it would start to make it better.

SUSAN Good.

PAUL There is a working party. I heard there was a working party looking into reform.

SUSAN Mmmmm?

PAUL Of the Cut. Within government. There's talk of reform. That's where it will happen. Not with the...students. There's a movement within government.

SUSAN Well...good.

PAUL I think the days are numbered.

SUSAN Well, don't tell me. Tell Stephen. He's the one to tell. I'm sure he'll be very interested. Will you talk to him on Saturday?

PAUL Of course.

SUSAN Well...good.

Is your fork clean?

PAUL I think so.

SUSAN Then please...eat.

They eat.

PAUL I'm a good man. At the end of the day I'm a good man.

SUSAN Of course you are.

Scene Three

A room. **PAUL** *and* **STEPHEN**.

PAUL You still look the same.

STEPHEN Yes?

PAUL To me. When I look at you you still look the same. Six months. Sicking up milk on my shoulder. Three years running through the grass. Eighteen. Off to the university. You always looked exactly the same to me.

STEPHEN Right.

PAUL And here you are. I look at you. And you still look... Nothing's changed. To me. Nothing's changed.

STEPHEN Dad.

PAUL But maybe you...what do you...how does it feel to you...?

STEPHEN Yeah.

PAUL Does it feel to you, does it feel to you that you've changed?

STEPHEN Yes.

PAUL Ah.

STEPHEN Yes it does.

PAUL Ah.

STEPHEN I feel as though I've changed.

PAUL Ah.

STEPHEN I feel as though, I feel...the world has changed. And I have changed.

PAUL Ah.

STEPHEN I feel that very strongly.

PAUL Ah. Ah. Ah. Ah. Youth. You're young.

STEPHEN Not so—

PAUL But still young. Still young enough. Still young enough not to see...

STEPHEN Yes?

PAUL It all comes round again. You do the same old stuff again and again and again.

STEPHEN No.

PAUL Oh yes. There's only so much shit in the pot and it's swilling around and if you're stuck in there long enough you'll spot the same old turds flying your way.

STEPHEN No.

PAUL That's the way it is. You listen to me. I'm an old cunt. And old cunts...old cunts know this sort of thing.

STEPHEN There's been a change.

PAUL Ha.

STEPHEN There's been a change. Everything's been turned on its head.

PAUL Black is white. Good is bad.

STEPHEN We're starting all over again. All of us together are starting together all over again.

PAUL Very good.

STEPHEN There's a chance together to start to build—

PAUL Fantastic. Terrific. I'm proud of you. Good with words. You're good with words. You can out-gibber the best. That's good. You were always like that. I can never quite... I always... suspected words. But you – straight into bed with the little fuckers and start banging away. That's good. Good. Good.

STEPHEN This really is a better world.

PAUL You know they turn the light on at five-thirty every morning? Every morning that fucking thing goes snap at half past five.

STEPHEN I'll have a word.

PAUL Apart from Sundays when – o blessed luxury! – it's six o'clock. We're indulged into six on a Sunday.

STEPHEN I'll talk to them. See if we can sort something out.

PAUL I don't want favours.

STEPHEN I'm listened to.

PAUL I don't need you pulling any favours for me. Don't you do any fucking favours on my account. I'm my own person. You're your own person. You don't want to be accused of, of, of...favours.

STEPHEN They're, we're not cruel.

PAUL They'll be watching out for that. You've always got to watch out for that. A new lot. Favours being pulled.

STEPHEN So you don't want me to try...?

PAUL I don't want you to try anything.

STEPHEN Alright. Alright.

PAUL What I want, what I want, what I want, what I want is for you to, to leave well alone.

STEPHEN Alright then.

PAUL Just...let it be.

STEPHEN Okay.

PAUL How's your mother?

STEPHEN She's fine.

PAUL Good. Good. Good.

STEPHEN Mina lost her baby.

PAUL The light goes off soon.

STEPHEN Mina had a baby. Inside her. Mina was pregnant. But then she lost the baby. Mother helped with the funeral. She dug.

PAUL Your mother?

STEPHEN Yes. She dug the hole.

PAUL Your mother dug the hole? Your mother dug a hole. Oh. Ha. Ha. Ha. I'm sorry. But that is fucking funny. Don't you think that is fucking funny?

STEPHEN I...

PAUL No. I'm sorry. Come on. The thought of your mother, the thought of your mother, the thought of her actually standing there with a spade and the earth and the... That is fucking funny, isn't it?

STEPHEN Is it?

PAUL Well, of course it is. Of course it is. What's... Can't you see the humour in...?

STEPHEN No.

PAUL Oh come on. Have you lost all...? Laugh for fuck's sake. Smile. Just let yourself...fuck. Fuck. Fuck.

STEPHEN Everything's changed. Everything's new. And in the new circumstances.

PAUL Yes? Yes?

STEPHEN And in the new circumstance it is quite appropriate, it is fitting, it is right that my mother, that your wife, should dig a hole.

PAUL Listen to yourself. Listen to yourself.

STEPHEN Dad.

PAUL Dig a hole? You sound comical. You sound...ridiculous. You sound fucking ridiculous.

STEPHEN To you maybe.

PAUL So get down off your high... Stop being so fucking pompous. And laugh.

STEPHEN That's not appropriate.

PAUL At yourself. At her. At me. If you like – come on. Rip the piss out of me. Rip the piss out of this whole shitty shebang.

STEPHEN I don't want to.

PAUL Christ's sake, fuck's sake...is there no humanity left? Do you none of you have a little fucking speck of humanity?

STEPHEN Don't you tell me – don't you tell me—

PAUL Alright.

STEPHEN About humanity. How can you tell me about humanity when you, you...?

PAUL Alright alright alright.

STEPHEN When you... The Cut. It's not me, it's not us... We never... Year after year... The instruments...

PAUL Yes.

STEPHEN Humanity? Humanity? Humanity?

PAUL You're right. Did you never think...?

STEPHEN No.

PAUL All the years and you never thought for a...?

STEPHEN No.

PAUL I was a good dad.

STEPHEN Yes.

PAUL I think your mother always knew.

STEPHEN She says not.

PAUL Everyday a little dance around each other because I suspected that she suspected.

STEPHEN She told the tribunal—

PAUL Sometimes it was actually quite fun.

STEPHEN She told the tribunal that there was never the faintest inkling.

PAUL Did she?

STEPHEN Yes.

PAUL Did she really?

STEPHEN Yes.

PAUL Well. Well. Well. Well I suppose she would. Each to their own, I suppose. You've got to save your own bacon when the chips are down, isn't that right?

STEPHEN I think she's telling the truth.

PAUL Oh no no no.

STEPHEN I could see it in her eyes.

PAUL No, no, no, because I spent the years, I had the years with so don't you...no. Lying.

STEPHEN No.

PAUL So – this is the bright new future. This is the new world. Kids who can't tell the difference between a lie and the truth. O son. O son, I would weep but there's no more fucking tears.

STEPHEN The tribunal cleared Mother.

PAUL Well, that's good.

STEPHEN But the house was in your name so...

PAUL Ah...

STEPHEN They're using it as a prison.

PAUL More prisons? A better world with more prisons?

STEPHEN There are certain temporary...

PAUL Yes, of course. Of course. Of course. Would you say I'm evil?

STEPHEN I...

PAUL No. Just look at me now. And would you say I'm evil.

STEPHEN I...

PAUL No. The heart. The gut. The soul. Listen. Listen. Listen to them now. And would you say...?

STEPHEN Yes.

PAUL ...that I'm evil?

STEPHEN Yes.

PAUL Ah.

STEPHEN Yes. There are systems of evil. There are acts of evil. There are people of evil. I say that there are all of these things. Yes. There is evil. And you are evil. You are it. You are my father and you are evil. That's what I say. Yes. Yes. Yes.

PAUL I see.

STEPHEN That's not personal...please don't take that the wrong...

PAUL It's alright.

STEPHEN Please. I'm sorry. I'm sorry.

PAUL No. Don't be. I bless you. Come here. Let me hold you.

STEPHEN No.

PAUL Please. Let me hold you so I can bless you for that.

> STEPHEN *moves to* PAUL. PAUL *holds him.*

Bless you for that. Bless you for that. Bless you for that.

> STEPHEN *moves away.*

You're honest. I'll give you that. We were never honest. Me. Your mother. The whole lot of us. We were never honest but you're...

STEPHEN I try.

PAUL So maybe it's better, yes? Maybe that's a bit better than before?

STEPHEN We like to think so.

PAUL Cold but honest. You are the future, my son.

STEPHEN And you...

PAUL And I'm...yeah, well, you're right about me. What you say. I'm...yes I am. Totally. In act and, and, and, and...soul. Totally.

STEPHEN But if you just...

PAUL No.

STEPHEN There is Forgiveness. That's what we...

PAUL No.

STEPHEN The Ministry of Forgiveness has hearings. You'll be heard. I can arrange for you to be heard. If you say what you've just said to me, you acknowledge, you can...

PAUL No.

STEPHEN There is a way forward.

PAUL I don't want to...no. I want punishment.

STEPHEN There are no—

PAUL I want to be paraded and scourged and feel the blood in my eyes and see the blades before me. I want to know that everyone sees my rottenness and is ready to cut it out.

STEPHEN What? What?

PAUL I am the dirt that needs to be destroyed so you can be purified.

STEPHEN What? Where do you get the...? No. No.

PAUL That's what I want.

STEPHEN That's so...old-fashioned.

PAUL Yes. Isn't it? Isn't it? Isn't it?

STEPHEN That doesn't happen anymore.

PAUL I know. I know. So. I'll sit it out. Lights on at five-thirty six days a week. Sunday indulgence. Sit it out 'til there's a new lot or this lot falls back on some of the old ways.

STEPHEN That isn't going to happen.

PAUL It always happens. Sooner or later. Sooner or later when the forgiveness is done there'll be scourging again and I'll be here. I'll be ready for it. It's what I deserve. I'm evil. It's what I deserve. The light's going to go. Any moment now that light's going to go blink and then there's going to be total blackness. So you had better piss off. Go on. Go on.

STEPHEN Dad.

PAUL You don't want to get stuck in the darkness. You go. There's a better world out there.

STEPHEN Goodbye.

End

PROPS

LIGHTING

SOUND EFFECTS

VISIT THE
SAMUEL FRENCH
BOOKSHOP
AT THE
ROYAL COURT THEATRE

Browse plays and theatre books, get expert advice and enjoy a coffee

Samuel French Bookshop
Royal Court Theatre
Sloane Square
London
SW1W 8AS
020 7565 5024

Shop from thousands of titles on our website

 samuelfrench.co.uk

 samuelfrenchltd

 samuel french uk

9 780573 116186